# Love, Feeling and Attraction

Archana Sai

Presentation by *BookLeaf Publishing*

Web: www.bookleafpub.com

E-mail: info@bookleafpub.com


ISBN: 9789357447850

First edition 2023

# DEDICATION

To my Fiancé Sai Prasad who helped to add more feelings and emotions to my thought process

# ACKNOWLEDGEMENT

Many Thanks to my Fiancé, Daddy, Mommy and Brother for being supportive and encouraging my creative writing works.

# The Way You Melt Me

Your voice melts away my ego
Your smile melts away my arrogance
You looking at me melt away my
self-centeredness
You in total melt me as a whole
May I forever be envelope in your web of love
and be together forever

# The Lucky Day

A cloudy day on the road full of dirt and dust
I(He) decided to go to church in search of peace
Then came the swirling winds and then the dust
in his eyes
"Damn..! Oh Damn must be an unlucky day"

Wiping the eyes and then the lucky strike
Wiping the eyes and then the beauty strikes
That's when he saw her getting down from the
car carrying such charm, delicacy and style
Blurred vision and then the dreamy day

Fogs cleared and the dullness gone, while she
became more visible
"Is that the thick bent eyebrows, just like a
rainbow?"
"Is that the long wavy hair, just like waves in
beach?"
"Is that a sharp pointed nose, just like a knife"?
"Is that a statue as a whole, just like made by a
chisel?"

There she goes wearing a white dress contrasting
the Whitish complexion
"Walking behind you and looking at you until
you took a seat
When everyone was busy in prayers and
thoughts
I ended up with my vision fixated on you"

# I Fell For You

A drizzling beautiful morning and here I am the
sizzling me,
Enjoying the Pleasant combination of warmth of
sun and chillness rain drops

My arms spread out and I was facing the sky
while he was looking at me.
I turned back and I caught him watching me.

Confident, bold and charming that he continued
to watch despite getting caught

May be too confident and too bold that he came
over to me
May be too charming when he smiled standing
beside me

It all started with him saying "you are beautiful
"and ended with me falling in love.

# I Miss You

I miss you every time when you are not around
I feel you even when you are far away

You are perfect just the way I wanted
Our souls connect the way we couldn't describe

When you hug me, your warmth feels like home
Now, it feels like I need to go back to home

I miss you when I look at your pictures
I kiss you even when you are far away

# Butterflies In My Tummy

This is not the first time I am going to meet you
in person,
But it feels like that every time I am about to
meet too.


Not sure whether it is due to,
Is it excitement?
Is it eagerness?
Is it little anxiety?
Is it because of Lots of Love?


When you are just about to come,
My anxiety will be at higher scales


When I just see you,
My heart races

When you come near and little closer,
I look at you well and much closer.


At that moment heart becomes calmer while,
Anxiety goes away
Excitement gets more boosts
Eagerness gets much more boost


I am left totally engulfed by your presence

# Remembering You

"So cold is the weather, that when I close my
eyes;

Cold air glides on my neck like a feather;

It feels like you are so near;

That when I open my eyes   you are not here;

I close my eyes again and again;

Cold air glides like a feather;"

# The Busy Bee

Those are the days you had time for me and I
had time for you

Today I still have time for you

I cherish the moments by just looking you when
you are busy with your favorite stuffs

Yet I secret wish at times you choose me over
anything else which you once did.

# The 1980's Love Letter

Looking at you makes me high,
Like I want to jump to the sky

Slowly you will become my drug,
That I can't live a day without your hug

We will be in love for long
Day and Night dancing to our own song
Making love all of my life with you

# The Secret Rendezvous

Every first glance at you in the atmosphere full
of romance,
My heart skips a beat and my mind secretly
wishes for a kiss

The closer you are, the lighter I become
Now that we go on a trip that I might catch your
lips

Without doubt I will be losing control of the
whole soul, living in my own world
Later when you leave me back, It would feel like
the warm breeze gone and little suffocating.

# The Heart Wins Over The Greedy Mind

So Intense are my feelings for you,
The fear of losing you smears my heart,
Pain seep into the heart making it heavy,
Pushing me deep into the ocean.

Going deeper and deeper.
With the constant battle between greedy mind
and painful heart,
Finally, the heart have won over me and my
greedy mind.

# The Perfect Love

Thy love is just so perfect that,
Thy love was able to open my heart and fetch
my soul

When thee hold my hand it feels heaven
When thee hug me it feels like peace
When thee cuddle me it feels like a safe nest

Thy love is just so perfect that,
I crave for it every time

Thy love is just so perfect that,
I am much at peace and safe as though in
heaven.

# Will You Stay?

We met again in the same street;
We broke up seven years ago.


We just met again in the same street;
We broke up in the heat of the fight.


What's this feel and now we are in reach,
Where's the anger? Where's the ego?


He asks for the coffee and it feels like first date
She is always hottie and it feels like the first
meet


Time is frozen and we stayed till the middle of
the night
She looked at the watch and it's time to go back


Her mind was like "Won't you ask me to stay
back?"

Her eyes are filled with Expectation, hesitation
and desperation.


His mind was like "Won't you stay back?"'
He looked into her eyes and chooses Silence.


Yet again they parted their ways with her tearful
eyes and his heavy heart.

# Passing Cloud

I came to party and I just say you
"Charming smile
Enchanting looks
You are not mine
You are just perfect"

I see you from a distance
"Dancing on the floor
Singing on the stage
You are not mine
So beautiful, like a flower"

# The Everyday Proposal

You (wife) had accident but here you are here
still elegant.
You lost memory and look at me like a mystery
You see me like a stranger and wonder if I am a
neighbor or perhaps a danger

I will tell you everything
I will walk you through everything that we went
together
I will be beside you this winter and make sure
you are not colder
One day you will fall in love and we will live
together again

# Obsession

Is it the addiction that I forget my inhibition or
Is it the closeness that I ignore my greediness


Your arms are my home without which I roam
Your presence keeps me at peace and moodiness
just cease


One complete day with you passes like
lightening
while every minute without you is less than less
than mundane


Your every touch melts me much that I started
longing for it,
That a mere thought of watching you up close
and returning without making love drains my
energy.

# We Will Always Be Together

Life will throw bricks at us
It will force us to think that it sucks
I will hold your hands tight
We both together will raise just like that kite

Hard days will be over and until that you can lay
on my shoulders
When you are at your lowest, still our love be
truest
Together we will cross the test of time
As we get older, out love gets even stronger

# We Finally Met

I am waiting at the table, not at all stable
With racing heart and chasing eyes
After all the texting and chatting, I am here
eager to meet you

Now I can see you at a distance
It feels like a dream while I silently scream
Happy, excited and nervous

You came close to my table and gave me a hand
shake
We spoke and you are like a chocolate cake
You ran your fingers through your hair

I am mesmerized, reenergized and very much
harmonized with you.

# The Nest

You make me feel so perfect
When we connect I forget myself

Your positive vibes crept into me
It swept away all the negative vibes

Those tight hugs are not just the tight hugs

That's my nest that I go back for a peace rest.

# His Presence

Here you are,
My heart is wherever you are.

Your presence brings in rejuvenescence
Your positive vibes is the feel good vibes

I radiate your energy which flows from you to me
your mere presence is a celebration

# The Wedding Photo shoot

We fought already we can't give a good pose,
We are upset and can't create artificial happy
pose.

Look at each other says the photographer
Keep looking for some more time as the
photographer shoots

When we look at each other, that's when the
anger starts to fade
Just a few more moments and the anger is
completely gone

Now that the album has arrived, so were the
memorable moments and beautiful pictures.

# The first Day To Now

It is the first day
Your hands shiver like a high school boy on a
first date

She fell in love on the first date
He fell in love, as months passed

Time passes by and the seasons Change,
While her passion and his commitment hold still

# Ever Since You Came Into My Life

Ever since you came into my life:
I am showered with all the love that I blossomed
into the flower
My soul is at heavenly peace that my in security
must cease
My heart is held when you hold my hands

May I ask myself?
Did the God created you just for me

# Reckless

Your absence leaves me breathless
In days to come, I shall be restless
Too anxious and I am feckless
Too Lonely and I am helpless
Each day seems endless
Finally I am reckless

# My Queen

She is my beautiful queen
I see her with her invisible crown
I will be loyal and I make sure she is forever
royal.

Such grace that I gladly will embrace
Such impression of elegance, but also the
intelligence
Such mildness, calmness and gentleness
Such beauty but she is also a cutie

Too perfect yet she choose me
I am not a king
With you I carry the king's pride

# Photograph

Feeling bored as I am alone
I just opened the phone


I went through all the pictures from winters,
dinners, and lustful linger
Full of memories, meaning events and stories to
tell ever since you sheltered me.